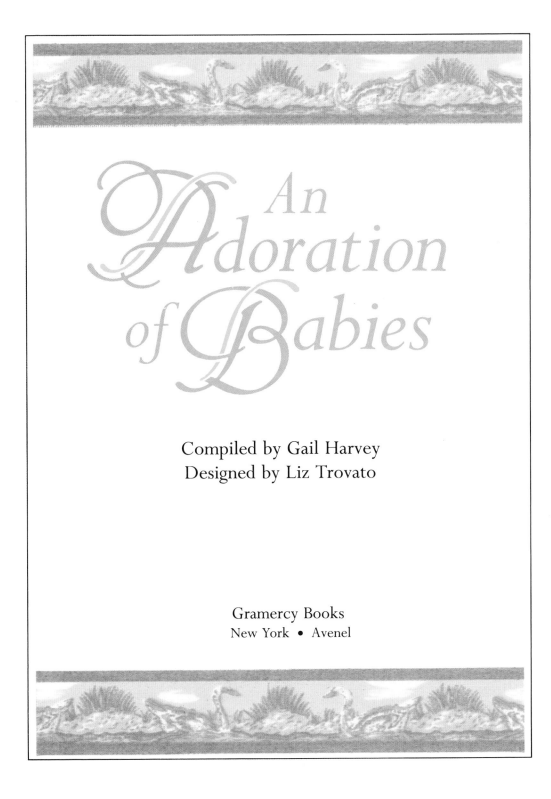

An Adoration of Babies

Compiled by Gail Harvey
Designed by Liz Trovato

Gramercy Books
New York • Avenel

Introduction and compilation
Copyright © 1994 by Outlet Book Company, Inc.
All rights reserved

Published by Gramercy Books,
distributed by Outlet Book Company, Inc.
a Random House Company,
40 Engelhard Avenue
Avenel, New Jersey 07001

Random House
New York • Toronto • London • Sydney • Auckland

Designed by Liz Trovato

Production Supervision: Roméo Enriquez

Printed and bound in the United States of America

Library of Congress Cataloging-in-Publication Data
An adoration of babies / compiled by Gail Harvey.
p. cm.
ISBN 0-517-09287-5
1. Infants—Literary collections. 2. Infants—Quotations,
maxims, etc. I. Harvey, Gail, 1942–
PN6071.I52A36   1993   92-37668
                                                  CIP

8 7 6 5 4 3 2 1

An Adoration of Babies

INTRODUCTION

A new baby is a miracle—a tiny human being with the enormous ability to captivate and delight. Each baby is a marvelous new beginning, a source of wonder, hope, and dreams. It is therefore not surprising that many of the world's great poets and novelists have extolled babies. Some have recorded treasured memories of their own children's babyhoods. Others tell of their enchantment with particular babies they have known.

An Adoration of Babies celebrates them in poems and prose, photographs and paintings. Leo Tolstoy describes the light of new joy when a baby is born and D.H. Lawrence writes of a young father's fascination with his new daughter. There are charming poems by Eugene Field, Lewis Carroll, Christina Rossetti, Henry Wadsworth Longfellow, and George Mac-Donald, as well as an amusing excerpt from Kate Douglas Wiggins's *Rebecca of Sunnybrook Farm*. Here you'll find Josiah Gilbert Holland's "Cradle Song," which begins with the question every adult has at some time asked: "What is the little one thinking about?" Mary Lamb writes of the difficulty in choosing just the right name for a newborn sister and Elizabeth Barrett Browning tells us about "Marion's Baby." Included, too, are many of Algernon Charles Swinburne's touching paeans to babyhood as well as lullabies by Alfred, Lord Tennyson, William Blake, and W.B. Yeats.

This beautiful book, with its beguiling photographs and illustrations by such wonderful artists as Arthur Rackham and Jessie Willcox Smith, will surely be enjoyed and treasured by everyone who has ever loved a baby.

GAIL HARVEY

New York
1994

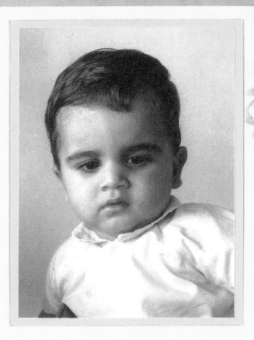

*Every baby born into the world
is a finer one than the last.*

CHARLES DICKENS

With her arms helplessly outstretched upon the quilt, unusually beautiful and calm she lay, gazing silently at him, trying unsuccessfully to smile.

And suddenly, out of the mysterious, terrible, and unearthly world in which he had been living for the last twenty-two hours, Levin felt himself instantaneously transported back to the old everyday world, but now radiant with the light of such new joy that it was insupportable. The taut strings snapped, and sobs and tears of joy that he had not in the least anticipated arose within him, with such force that they shook his whole body and long prevented his speaking.

Falling on his knees by her bedside he held his wife's hand to his lips, kissing it, and that hand, by a feeble movement of the fingers, replied to the kisses. And meanwhile at the foot of the bed, like a flame above a lamp, flickered in Mary Vlasevna's skillful hands the life of a human being who had never before existed: a human being who, with the same right and the same importance to himself, would live and would procreate others like himself.

"Alive! Alive! And a boy! Don't be anxious," Levin heard Mary Vlasevna say, as she slapped the baby's back with a shaking hand.

"Mama, is it true?" asked Kitty. . . .

And amid the silence, as a positive answer to the mother's question, a voice quite unlike all the restrained voices that had been speaking in the room made itself heard. It was a bold, insolent voice that had no consideration for anything, it was the cry of the new human being who had so incomprehensibly appeared from some unknown realm.

FROM "ANNA KARENINA" BY LEO TOLSTOY

Last night the Stork came stalking,
And, Stork, beneath your wing
Lay, lapped in dreamless slumber,
The tiniest little thing!
From Babyland, out yonder
Beside a silver sea,
You brought a priceless treasure
As gift to mine and me!

Last night a babe awakened,
And, babe, how strange and new,
Must seem the home and people
The Stork has brought you to;

And yet methinks you like them—
You neither stare nor weep,
But closer to my dear one
You cuddle, and you sleep!

Last night my heart grew fonder—
O happy heart of mine.
Sing of the inspirations
That round my pathway shine!
And sing your sweetest love song
To this dear nestling wee
The Stork from Way-Out-Yonder
Hath brought to mine and me.

EUGENE FIELD

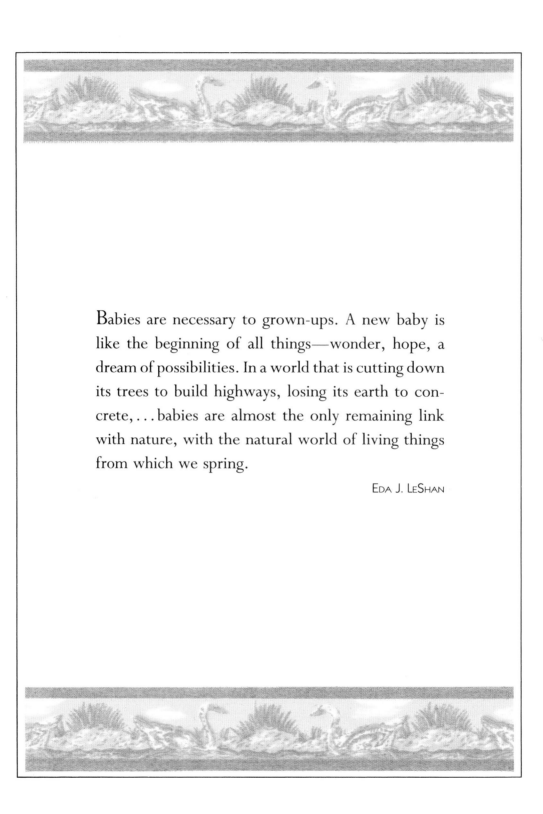

Babies are necessary to grown-ups. A new baby is
like the beginning of all things—wonder, hope, a
dream of possibilities. In a world that is cutting down
its trees to build highways, losing its earth to con-
crete, . . . babies are almost the only remaining link
with nature, with the natural world of living things
from which we spring.

EDA J. LeShan

A baby is God's opinion
that the world should go on.

CARL SANDBURG

Each mother's nurturing breast
Feeds a flower of bliss,
Beyond all blessing
Blest.

ALGERNON CHARLES SWINBURNE

Where did you come from, baby dear?
Out of the everywhere into the here.

Where did you get those eyes so blue?
Out of the sky as I came through.

What makes the light in them sparkle and spin?
Some of the starry spikes left in.

Where did you get that little tear?
I found it waiting when I got here.

What makes your forehead so smooth and high?
A soft hand strok'd it as I went by.

What makes your cheek like a warm white rose?
I saw something better than anyone knows.

Whence that three-corner'd smile of bliss?
Three angels gave me at once a kiss.

Where did you get this pearly ear?
God spoke, and it came out to hear.

Where did you get those arms and hands?
Love made itself into bonds and bands.

Feet, whence did you come, you darling things?
From the same box as the cherubs' wings.

How did they all just come to be you?
God thought about me, and so I grew.

But how did you come to us, you dear?
God thought about you, and so I am here.

GEORGE MACDONALD

Whenever a little child is born
All night a soft wind rocks the corn;
One more buttercup wakes to the morn,
  Somewhere, somewhere.

One more rosebud shy will unfold,
One more grass blade push through the mold,
One more bird song the air will hold,
  Somewhere, somewhere.

Agnes Carter Mason

She named the infant "Pearl," as being of a great price—purchased with all she had—her mother's only treasure!...By its perfect shape, its vigor, and its natural dexterity in the use of all its untried limbs, the infant was worthy to have been brought forth in Eden; worthy to have been left there, to be the plaything of the angels, after the world's first parents were driven out....Pearl's aspect was imbued with a spell of infinite variety; in this one child there were many children, comprehending the full scope between the wildflower prettiness of a peasant-baby, and the pomp, in little, of an infant princess.

FROM "THE SCARLET LETTER" BY NATHANIEL HAWTHORNE

When the first baby laughed
for the first time, the laugh broke
into a thousand pieces and they
all went skipping about, and
that was the beginning of fairies.

FROM "PETER PAN" BY JAMES M. BARRIE

Monday's child is fair of face,

Tuesday's child is full of grace,

Wednesday's child

is full of woe,

Thursday's child has far to go,

Friday's child is loving and giving,

Saturday's child

works hard for a living,

And the child that is born on

the Sabbath day

Is bonny and blithe,

and good and gay.

MORNING SONG

Baby darling, wake and see,
    Morning's here, my little rose;
Open eyes and smile at me
    Ere I clasp and kiss you close.
          Baby darling, smile! for then
          Mother sees the sun again.

Baby darling, sleep no more!
    All the other flowers have done
With their sleeping—you, my flower,
    Are the only sleepy one;
          All the pink-frilled daisies shout:
          "Bring our little sister out!"

Baby darling, in the sun
    Birds are singing, sweet and shrill;
And my bird's the only one
    That is nested softly still.
          Baby—if you only knew,
          All the birds are calling you!

Baby darling, all is bright,
    God has brought the sunshine here;
And the sleepy silent night
    Comes back soon enough, my dear!
          Wake, my darling, night is done,
          Sunbeams call my little one!

                        E. NESBIT

SONG

Oh, baby, baby, baby dear,
We lie alone together here;
The snowy gown and cap and sheet
With lavender are fresh and sweet;
Through half-closed blinds the roses peer
To see and love you, baby dear.

We are so tired, we like to lie
Just doing nothing, you and I,
Within the darkened quiet room.
The sun sends dusk rays through the gloom,
Which is no gloom since you are here,
My little life, my baby dear.

Soft sleepy mouth so vaguely pressed
Against your new-made mother's breast.
Soft little hands in mine I fold,
Soft little feet I kiss and hold,
Round, soft, smooth head and tiny ear,
All mine, my own, my baby dear.

And he we love is far away!
But he will come some happy day,
You need but me, and I can rest
At peace with you beside me pressed.
There are no questions, longings vain,
No murmuring, nor doubt, nor pain,
Only content and we are here,
　　My baby dear.

E. Nesbit

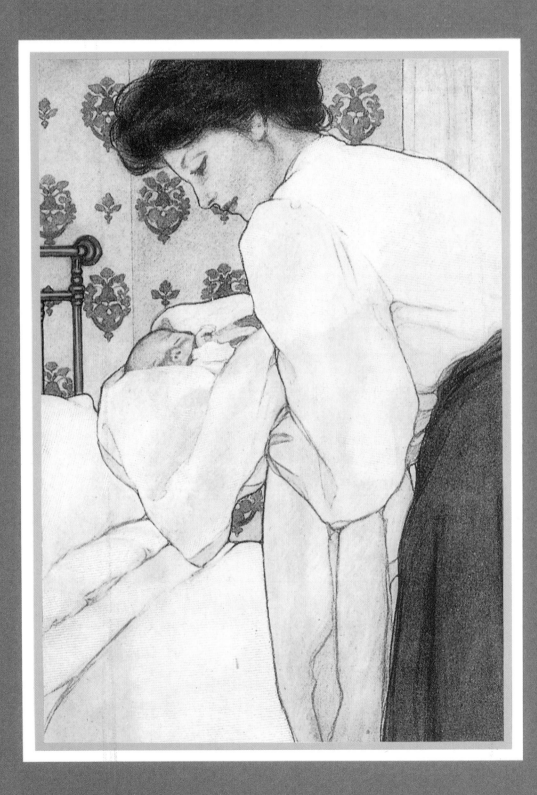

MARION'S BABY

There he lay upon his back,
The yearling creature, warm and moist with life
To the bottom of his dimples—and to the ends
Of the lovely tumbled curls about his face;
For since he had been covered over-much
To keep him from the light-glare, both his cheeks
Were hot and scarlet as the first live rose
The shepherd's heart-blood ebbed away into
The faster for his love. And love was here
As instant; in the pretty baby mouth,
Shut close as if for dreaming that it sucked,
The little naked feet, drawn up the way
Of nestled birdlings; everything so soft
And tender—to the tiny holdfast hands
Which, closing on a finger into sleep,
Had kept a mold of't.

ELIZABETH BARRETT BROWNING

*H*ush-a-bye, baby,
   on the tree top,
When the wind blows,
   the cradle will rock;
When the bough breaks
   the cradle will fall,
Down will come baby,
   cradle and all.

What is the little one thinking about?
Very wonderful things, no doubt;
Unwritten history!
Unfathomed mystery!
Yet he chuckles, and crows, and nods, and winks,
As if his head were as full of kinks
And curious riddles as any sphinx!
Warped by colic, and wet by tears,
Punctured by pins, and tortured by fears,
Our little nephew will lose two years;
And he'll never know
Where the summers go;
He need not laugh, for he'll find it so.

Who can tell what a baby thinks?
Who can follow the gossamer links
By which the manikin feels his way

Out from the shore of the great unknown,
Blind, and wailing, and alone,
   Into the light of day?
Out from the shore of the unknown sea,
Tossing in pitiful agony;
Of the unknown sea that reels and rolls,
Specked with the barks of little souls,
Barks that were launched on the other side,
And slipped from heaven on an ebbing tide!
   What does he think of his mother's eyes?
What does he think of his mother's hair?
   What of the cradle-roof, that flies
Forward and backward through the air?

What does he think of his mother's breast,
Bare and beautiful, smooth and white,
Seeking it ever with fresh delight,
   Cup of his life, and couch of his rest?
What does he think when her quick embrace
Presses his hand and buries his face
Deep where the heartthrobs sink and swell,
With a tenderness she can never tell,
   Though she murmur the words
   Of all the birds,
Words she has learned to murmur well?
   Now he thinks he'll go to sleep!
   I can see the shadow creep
   Over his eyes in soft eclipse,
   Over his brow and over his lips,
   Out to his little fingertips!
   Softly sinking, down he goes!
   Down he goes! down he goes!
   See! he's hushed in sweet repose.

                    JOSIAH GILBERT HOLLAND

I know a baby, such a baby,
Round blue eyes and cheeks of pink,
Such an elbow furrowed with dimples.
Such a wrist where creases sink.

"Cuddle and love me, cuddle and love me,"
Crows the mouth of coral pink:
Oh the bald head, and oh the sweet lips,
And oh the sleepy eyes that wink!

CHRISTINA ROSSETTI

Choosing a Name

I have got a newborn sister;
I was nigh the first that kissed her.
When the nursing woman brought her
To Papa, his infant daughter,
How Papa's dear eyes did glisten!
She will shortly be to christen;
And Papa has made the offer,
I shall have the naming of her.
Now I wonder what would please her,
Charlotte, Julia, or Louisa?
Ann and Mary, they're too common;
Joan's too formal for a woman;
Edith's pretty, but that looks
Better in old English books;
Ellen's left off long ago;
Blanche is out of fashion now.
None that I have named as yet
Are so good as Margaret.
Emily is neat and fine;
What do you think of Caroline?
How I'm puzzled and perplexed
What to choose or think of next!
I am in a little fever
Lest the name that I should give her
Should disgrace her or defame her;
I will leave Papa to name her.

Mary Lamb

A New Baby

A baby came to our house
  Not very long ago,
And Father says we'll keep it here,
  'Cause Mother loves it so.

I didn't understand at first
  My heart felt very sore.
It seemed to me that Mother would
  N't love me any more.

But Mother took me in her arms,
    Just like she used to do
And told me that a mother's heart
    Was big enough for two,

And that she loved me just the same.
    Because of this, you see:
The place I have in Mother's heart
    Is always kept for me.

ARTHUR ALDEN KNIPES

A baby is an angel
whose wings decrease
as his legs increase.

FRENCH PROVERB

Three Weeks Old

Three weeks since there was no such rose in being;
  Now may eyes made dim with deep delight
See how fair it is, laugh with love, and seeing
  Praise the chance that bids us bless the sight.

Three weeks old, and a very rose of roses,
  Bright and sweet as love is sweet and bright.
Heaven and earth, till a man's life wanes and closes,
  Show not life or love a lovelier sight.

Three weeks past have renewed the rose-bright creature
  Day by day with life, and night by night.
Love, though fain of its every faultless feature,
  Finds not words to match the silent night.

ALGERNON CHARLES SWINBURNE

TO A CHILD

By what astrology of fear or hope
Dare I to cast thy horoscope!
Like the new moon thy life appears;
A little strip of silver light,
And widening outward into night
The shadowy disk of future years;
And yet upon its outer rim,
A luminous circle, faint and dim,
And scarcely visible to us here,
Rounds and completes the perfect sphere;
A prophecy and intimation,
A pale and feeble adumbration,
Of the great world of light, that lies
Behind all human destinies.

HENRY WADSWORTH LONGFELLOW

THE MOTHER'S HOPE

Is there, when the winds are singing
    In the happy summer time,
When the raptured air is ringing
With Earth's music heavenward springing,
    Forest chirp, and village chime,
Is there, of the sounds that float
Unsighingly, a single note
Half so sweet, and clear, and wild,
As the laughter of a child?

Listen! and be now delighted:
    Morn hath touched her golden strings;
Earth and Sky their vows have plighted;
Life and Light are reunited
    Amid countless carolings;
Yet, delicious as they are,
There's a sound that's sweeter far,
One that makes the heart rejoice
More than all—the human voice!

Organ finer, deeper, clearer,
    Though it be a stranger's tone,
Than the winds or waters dearer,
More enchanting to the hearer,
    For it answereth to his own.
But, of all its witching words,
Those are sweetest, bubbling wild
Through the laughter of a child.

Harmonies from time-touched towers,
    Haunted strains from rivulets,
Hum of bees among the flowers,
Rustling leaves, and silver showers,
    These, erelong, the ear forgets;
But in mine there is a sound
Ringing on the whole year round,
Heart-deep laughter that I heard
Ere my child could speak a word.

Ah! 't was heard by ear far purer,
    Fondlier formed to catch the strain,
Ear of one whose love is surer,
Hers, the mother, the endurer
    Of the deepest share of pain;
Hers the deepest bliss to treasure
Memories of that cry of pleasure;
Hers to hoard, a lifetime after,
Echoes of that infant laughter.

'T is a mother's large affection
    Hears with a mysterious sense,
Breathings that evade detection,
Whisper faint, and fine inflection,
    Thrill in her with powers intense.
Childhood's honeyed words untaught
Hiveth she in loving thought,
Tones that never thence depart;
For she listens—with her heart.

LAMAN BLANCHARD

From the first, the baby stirred in the young father a deep, strong emotion he dared scarcely acknowledge, it was so strong and came out of the dark of him. When he heard the child cry, a terror possessed him, because of the answering echo from the unfathomed distances in himself. Must he know in himself such distances, perilous and imminent?

He had the infant in his arms, he walked backwards and forwards troubled by the crying of his own flesh and blood. This was his own flesh and blood crying! His soul rose against the voice suddenly breaking out from him, from the distances in him. . . .

He became accustomed to the child, he knew how to lift and balance the little body. The baby had a beautiful, rounded head that moved him passionately. He would have fought to the last drop to defend that exquisite, perfect round head.

He learned to know the little hands and feet, the strange, unseeing, golden-brown eyes, the mouth that opened only to cry, or to suck, or to show a queer, toothless laugh. He could almost understand even the dangling legs, which at first had created in him a feeling of aversion. They could kick in their queer little way, they had their own softness.

One evening, suddenly, he saw the tiny, living thing rolling naked in the mother's lap, and he was sick, it was so utterly helpless and vulnerable and extraneous; in a world of hard surfaces and varying altitudes, it lay vulnerable and naked at every point. Yet it was quite blithe. And yet, in its blind, awful crying, was there not the blind, far-off terror of its own vulnerable nakedness, the terror of being so utterly delivered over, helpless at every point. He could not bear to hear it crying. His heart strained and stood on guard against the whole universe.

But he waited for the dread of these days to pass; he saw the joy coming. He saw the lovely, creamy, cool little ear of the baby, a bit of dark hair rubbed to a bronze floss, like bronze-dust. And he waited, for the child to become his, to look at him and answer him.

It had a separate being, but it was his own child. His flesh and blood vibrated to it. He caught the baby to his breast with his passionate, clapping laugh. And the infant knew him.

As the newly opened, newly dawned eyes looked at him, he wanted them to perceive him, to recognize him. Then he was verified. The child knew him, a queer contortion of laughter came on its face for him. He caught it to his breast, clapping with a triumphant laugh.

The golden-brown eyes of the child gradually lit up and dilated at the sight of the dark-glowing face of the youth. It knew its mother better, it wanted its mother more. But the brightest, sharpest little ecstasy was for the father.

It began to be strong, to move vigorously and freely, to make sounds like words. It was a baby girl now. Already it knew his strong hands, it exulted in his strong clasp, it laughed and crowed when he played with it.

FROM "THE RAINBOW" BY D. H. LAWRENCE

HERSE

When grace is given us ever to behold
    A child some sweet months old,
Love, laying across our lips his finger, saith,
    Smiling, with bated breath,
Hush! for the holiest thing that lives is here,
    And heaven's own heart how near!
How dare we, that may gaze not on the sun,
    Gaze on this verier one?
Heart, hold thy peace; eyes, be cast down for shame;
    Lips, breathe not yet its name.
In heaven they know what name to call it; we,
    How should we know? For, see!
The adorable sweet living marvelous
    Strange light that lightens us
Who gaze, desertless of such glorious grace,
    Full in a babe's warm face!
All roses that the morning rears are nought,
    All stars not worth a thought,
Set this one star against them, or suppose
    As rival this one rose.
What price could pay with earth's whole weight of gold
    One least flushed roseleaf's fold
Of all this dimpling store of smiles that shine
    From each warm curve and line,

Each charm of flower-sweet flesh, to reillume
  The dappled rose-red bloom
Of all its dainty body, honey-sweet
  Clenched hands and curled-up feet,
That on the roses of the dawn have trod
  As they came down from God,
And keep the flush and color that the sky
  Takes when the sun comes nigh,
And keep the likeness of the smile their grace
  Evoked on God's own face
When, seeing this work of his most heavenly mood,
  He saw that it was good?
For all its warm sweet body seems one smile,
  And mere men's love too vile
To meet it, or with eyes that worship dims
  Read o'er the little limbs,
Read all the book of all their beauties o'er,
  Rejoice, revere, adore,
Bow down and worship each delight in turn,
  Laugh, wonder, yield, and yearn.
But when our trembling kisses dare, yet dread,
  Even to draw nigh its head,
And touch, and scarce with touch or breath surprise
  Its mild miraculous eyes
Out of their viewless vision—O, what then,
  What may be said of men?

What speech may name a newborn child? what word
    Earth ever spake or heard?
The best men's tongue that ever glory knew
    Called that a drop of dew
Which from the breathing creature's kindly womb
    Came forth in blameless bloom.

We have no word, as had those men most high,
    To call a baby by.
Rose, ruby, lily, pearl of stormless seas—
    A better word than these,
A better sign it was than flower or gem
    That love revealed to them:

They knew that whence comes light or quickening flame,
    Thence only this thing came,
And only might be likened of our love
    To somewhat born above,
Not even to sweetest things dropped else on earth,
    Only to dew's own birth.

Nor doubt we but their sense was heavenly true,
    Babe, when we gaze on you,
A dewdrop out of heaven whose colors are
    More bright than sun or star,
As now, ere watching love dare fear or hope,
    Lips, hands, and eyelids ope,
And all your life is mixed with earthly heaven.
    O child, what news from heaven?

ALGERNON CHARLES SWINBURNE

A Baby's Eyes

A baby's eyes, ere speech begin,
*   Ere lips learn words or sighs,*
Bless all things bright enough to win
*   A baby's eyes.*

Love, while the sweet thing laughs and lies,
*   And sleep flows out and in,*
Sees perfect in them Paradise.

Their glance might cast out pain and sin,
*   Their speech make dumb the wise,*
By mute glad godhead felt within
*   A baby's eyes.*

ALGERNON CHARLES SWINBURNE

A Baby's Hands

A baby's hands, like rosebuds furled
    Whence yet no leaf expands,
Ope if you touch, though close upcurled,
    A baby's hands.

Then, fast as warriors grip their brands
    When battle's bolt is hurled,
They close, clenched hard like tightening bands.

No rosebuds yet by dawn impearled
    Match, even in loveliest lands,
The sweetest flowers in all the world—
    A baby's hands.

ALGERNON CHARLES SWINBURNE

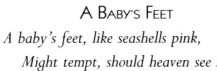

A Baby's Feet

A baby's feet, like seashells pink,
Might tempt, should heaven see meet,
An angel's lips to kiss, we think,
A baby's feet.

Like rose-hued sea-flowers toward the heat
They stretch and spread and wink
Their ten soft buds that part and meet.

No flower-bells that expand and shrink
Gleam half so heavenly sweet
As shine on life's untrodden brink
A baby's feet.

ALGERNON CHARLES SWINBURNE

MY BABY

My baby has a mottled fist,
My baby has a neck in creases;
My baby kisses and is kissed,
For he's the very thing for kisses.

CHRISTINA ROSSETTI

To Charlotte Pulteney

Timely blossom, Infant fair,
Fondling of a happy pair,
Every morn and every night
Their solicitous delight,
Sleeping, waking, still at ease,
Pleasing, without skill to please;
Little gossip, blithe and hale,
Tattling many a broken tale,
Singing many a tuneless song,
Lavish of a heedless tongue;

Simple maiden, void of art,
Babbling out the very heart,
Yet abandoned to thy will,
Yet imagining no ill;
Yet too innocent to blush;
Like the linnet in the bush
To the mother-linnet's note
Moduling her slender throat;
Chirping forth thy petty joys,
Wanton in the change of toys,

Like the linnet green, in May
Flitting to each bloomy spray;
Wearied then and glad of rest,
Like the linnet in the nest;
This thy present happy lot,
This in time will be forgot:
Other pleasures, other cares,
Ever busy Time prepares;
And thou shalt in thy daughter see,
This picture, once, resembled thee.

AMBROSE PHILIPS

There is no finer investment
for any community
than putting milk into babies.

WINSTON CHURCHILL

Father asked us what was God's noblest work. Anna said *men*, but I said *babies*. Men are often bad; babies never are.

Louisa May Alcott,
in her diary when
she was eleven years old

In a Garden

Baby, see the flowers!
—Baby sees
Fairer things than these,
Fairer though they be than dreams of ours.

Baby, hear the birds!
—Baby knows
Better songs than those,
Sweeter though they sound than sweetest words.

Baby, see the moon!
—Baby's eyes
Laugh to watch it rise,
Answering light with love and night with noon.

Baby, hear the sea!
—Baby's face
Takes a graver grace,
Touched with wonder what the sound may be.

Baby, see the star!
—Baby's hand
Opens, warm and bland,
Calm in claim of all things fair that are.

Baby, hear the bells!
—Baby's head
Bows, as ripe for bed,
Now the flowers curl round and close their cells.

Baby, flower of light,
Sleep, and see
Brighter dreams than we,
Till good day shall smile away good night.

ALGERNON CHARLES SWINBURNE

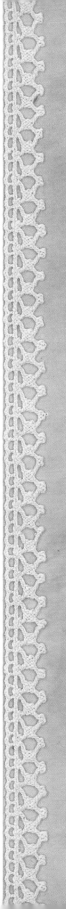

Life in the brick house had gone on more placidly of late, for Rebecca was honestly trying to be more careful in the performance of her tasks and duties as well as more quiet in her plays, and she was slowly learning the power of the soft answer in turning away wrath.

Miranda had not had, perhaps, quite as many opportunities in which to lose her temper, but it is only just to say that she had not fully availed herself of all that had offered themselves.

There had been one outburst of righteous wrath occasioned by Rebecca's over hospitable habits. On a certain Friday afternoon she asked her Aunt Miranda if she might take half her bread and milk upstairs to a friend.

"What friend have you got up there, for pity's sake?" demanded Aunt Miranda.

"The Simpson baby, come to stay over Sunday; that is, if you're willing, Mrs. Simpson says she is. Shall I bring her down and show her? She's dressed in an old dress of Emma Jane's and she looks sweet."

"You can bring her down, but you can't show her to me! You can smuggle her out the way you smuggled her in and take her back to her mother. Where on earth do you get your notions, borrowing a baby for Sunday!"

"You're so used to a house without a baby you don't know how dull it is," sighed Rebecca resignedly, as she moved towards the door, "but at the farm there was always a nice fresh one to play with and cuddle. There were too many, but that's not half as bad as none at all. Well, I'll take her back. She'll be dreadfully disappointed and so will Mrs. Simpson. She was planning to go to Milltown."

"She can un-plan then," observed Miss Miranda.

"Perhaps I can go up there and take care of the baby?" suggested Rebecca. "I brought her home so 't I could do my Saturday work just the same."

"You've got enough to do right here, without any borrowed babies to make more steps. Now, no answering back, just give the child some supper and carry it home where it belongs."

"You don't want me to go down the front way, hadn't I better just come through this room and let you look at her?

She has yellow hair and big blue eyes! Mrs. Simpson says she takes after her father.''

Miss Miranda smiled acidly as she said she couldn't take after her father, for he'd take anything there was before she got there!

Aunt Jane was in the linen closet upstairs, sorting out the clean sheets and pillow cases for Saturday, and Rebecca sought comfort from her.

''I brought the Simpson baby home, Aunt Jane, thinking it would help us over a dull Sunday, but Aunt Miranda won't let her stay. Emma Jane has the promise of her next Sunday and Alice Robinson the next. Mrs. Simpson wanted I should have her first because I've had so much experience in babies. Come in and look at her sitting up in my bed, Aunt Jane! Isn't she lovely? She's the fat, gurgly kind, not thin and fussy like some babies, and I thought I was going to have her to undress and dress twice each day. Oh dear! I wish I could have a printed book with everything set down in it that I *could* do, and then I wouldn't get disappointed so often.''

''No book could be printed that would fit you, Rebecca,'' answered Aunt Jane, ''for nobody could imagine beforehand the things you'd want to do. Are you going to carry that heavy child home in your arms?''

''No, I'm going to drag her in the little soap wagon. Come, baby! Take your thumb out of your mouth and come to ride with Becky in your go-cart.'' She stretched out her strong young arms to the crowing baby, sat down in a chair with the child, turned her upside down unceremoniously, took from her waistband and scornfully flung away a crooked pin, walked with her (still in a highly reversed position) to the bureau, selected a large safety pin, and proceeded to attach her brief red flannel petticoat to a sort of shirt that she wore. Whether flat on her stomach, or heads down, heels in the air, the Simpson baby knew she was in the hands of an expert, and continued gurgling placidly while Aunt Jane regarded the pantomime with a kind of dazed awe.

"Bless my soul, Rebecca," she ejaculated, "it beats all how handy you are with babies!"

"I ought to be; I've brought up three and a half of 'em," Rebecca responded cheerfully, pulling up the infant Simpson's stockings.

"I should think you'd be fonder of dolls than you are," said Jane.

"I do like them, but there's never any change in a doll. It's always the same everlasting old doll, and you have to make believe it's cross or sick, or it loves you, or can't bear you. Babies are more trouble, but nicer."

FROM "REBECCA OF SUNNYBROOK FARM"
BY KATE DOUGLAS WIGGINS

THE BABY'S DANCE

Dance, little baby, dance up high,
Never mind baby, Mother is by;
Crow and caper, caper and crow,
There little baby, there you go:
Up to the ceiling, down to the ground,
Backwards and forwards, round and round.
Then dance, little baby, and Mother shall sing,
With the merry gay coral, ding, ding, a-ding, ding.

ANN TAYLOR

Say, what is the spell, when her fledglings are cheeping,
That lures the bird home to her nest?
Or wakes the tired mother whose infant is weeping,
To cuddle and croon it to rest?
What the magic that charms the glad babe in her arms
Till it cooes with the voice of a dove?
'Tis a secret, and so let us whisper it low—
And the name of the secret is Love!
For I think it is Love,
For I feel it is Love,
For I'm sure it is nothing but Love!

LEWIS CARROLL

Her First Bonnet

A bonnet of linen,
   A bonnet of lace,
A bonnet for baby
   To cover her face.
A bonnet so big that
   Without any doubt,
One sees but a bonnet
   A-bobbin' about.

Arthur Alden Knipe

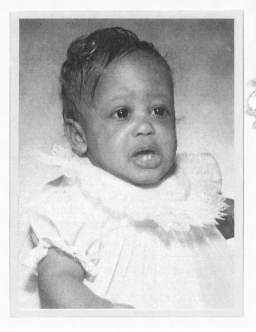

*W*ell, I just got a tooth today,
I really don't know why.
It seems to make my mother glad
But only makes me cry!

AUTHOR UNKNOWN

First Footsteps

A little way, more soft and sweet
　　Than fields aflower with May,
A babe's feet, venturing, scarce complete
　　A little way.

　　Eyes full of dawning day
Look up for Mother's eyes to meet,
　　Too blithe for song to say.

Glad as the golden spring to greet
　　Its first live leaflet's play,
Love, laughing, leads the little feet
　　A little way.

Algernon Charles Swinburne

A sweet child
is the sweetest thing in nature.

CHARLES LAMB

Why should May remember
    March, if March forget
The days that began with December,
    The nights that a frost could fret?

All their griefs are done with
    Now the bright months bless
Fit souls to rejoice in the sun with,
    Fit heads for the wind's caress;

Souls of children quickening
    With the whole world's mirth,
Heads closelier than field-flowers thickening
    That crowd and illuminate earth,

Now that May's call musters
    Files of baby bands
To marshal in joyfuller clusters
    Than the flowers that encumber their hands.

ALGERNON CHARLES SWINBURNE

LULLABY

Sweet and low, sweet and low,
Wind of the western sea,
Low, low, breathe and blow,
Wind of the western sea!
Over the rolling waters go,
Come from the dying moon, and blow,
Blow him again to me;
While my pretty one, while my pretty one, sleeps.

Sleep and rest, sleep and rest,
Father will come to thee soon,
Rest, rest, on Mother's breast,
Father will come to thee soon;
Father will come to his babe in the nest,
Silver sails all out of the west
Under the silver moon:
Sleep, my little one, sleep, my pretty one, sleep.

ALFRED, LORD TENNYSON

A Cradle Song

Sweet dreams form a shade,
O'er my lovely infant's head.
Sweet dreams of pleasant streams.
By happy silent moony beams.

Sweet sleep with soft down,
Weave thy brows an infant crown.
Sweet sleep, Angel mild,
Hover o'er my happy child.

Sweet smiles in the night,
Hover over my delight.
Sweet smiles, Mother smiles
All the livelong night beguiles.

Sweet moans, dovelike sighs,
Chase not slumber from thy eyes.
Sweet moans, sweeter smiles.
All the dovelike moans beguiles.

Sleep, sleep, happy child.
All creation slept and smil'd.
Sleep, sleep, happy sleep.
While o'er thee thy mother weep.

WILLIAM BLAKE

Some things go to sleep in such a funny way.
Little birds stand on one leg and tuck their head away.

Chickens do the same standing on their perch;
Little mice lie soft and still as if they were in a church.

Kittens curl up close in such a funny ball,
Horses hang their sleepy heads and stand still in a stall;

Sometimes dogs stretch out, or curl up in a heap;
Cows lie down upon their sides when they would go to sleep.

But little babies dear are snugly tucked in beds,
Warm with blankets, all so soft, and pillows for their heads.

Bird and beast and babe—I wonder which of all
Dream the dearest dreams that down from dreamland fall!

ALFRED, LORD TENNYSON

Sleep, baby, sleep!
Thy father's watching the sheep,
Thy mother's shaking the dreamland tree,
And down drops a little dream for thee.
Sleep, baby, sleep.

ELIZABETH PRENTISS

A Cradle Song

The angels are bending
   Above your white bed,
They weary of tending
   The souls of the dead.

God smiles in high heaven
   To see you so good,
The old planets seven
   Grow gay with his mood.

I kiss you and kiss you,
   With arms round my own,
Ah, how shall I miss you,
   When, dear, you have grown.

W. B. Yeats

Life's aspirations
come in the guise of children.

RABINDRANATH TAGORE

WHERE·CHILDREN·ARE·NOT·HEAVEN·IS·NOT

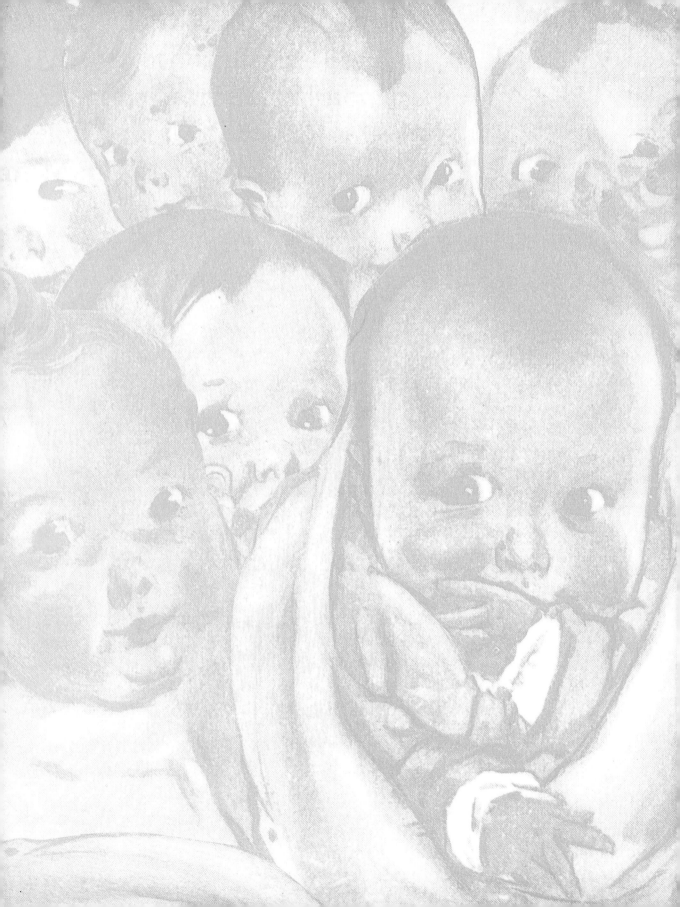

SUSAN WEAVER